Human Tissue

Hilary Menos

smith|doorstop

Published 2020 by
Smith|Doorstop Books
The Poetry Business
Campo House,
54 Campo Lane,
Sheffield S1 2EG

ISBN 978-1-912196-78-4
Typeset by Utter
Printed by People for Print, Sheffield

Smith|Doorstop books are a member of Inpress:
www.inpressbooks.co.uk.

Distributed by NBN International, Airport Business Centre,
10 Thornbury Road Plymouth PL6 7PP

The Poetry Business gratefully acknowledges the support of
Arts Council England.

A Note on *Human Tissue*

A prose version of this book might be called "What they don't tell you about transplants". The public likes to imagine that organ transplant is a universal blessing and salvation. The truth is these are early days of the science and many patients suffer in the name of progress.

Hilary Menos's son Linus, who suffered from kidney failure, had a "successful" transplant, aged 17, of one of his mother's kidneys – "successful" in that it took quickly and functioned well to start with. What nobody told him about, or her, were the headaches, the itching and the permanent shaking. Aged 19, Linus had a massive rejection episode. They had to remove his mother's kidney and he is now on dialysis.

Such is the horrific background to a life and death thriller of a poetry book, if I can put it crudely. A gifted poet, whose earlier collection, *Berg*, won a Forward prize, Menos writes the kind of English that operates like a surgeon's knife on its material, with the difference that it has a sure grasp of the metaphorical implications and potential of its subject matter. Her determination to understand every last detail of the failure and replacement of the body's second most complex organ may be a revelation to doctors and public alike. Her readers will surely be impressed by the eloquence and beauty of her insight.

– Hugo Williams

Contents

for Linus

The Mud Man

The Mud Man squats in the copse,
his one long leg slung out like a telegraph pole.
From the back he looks like a minotaur having a massage.
From the side he looks like a bull with a bone in its mouth.
From the front he looks like a gymnast doing the splits,
a one-legged gymnast with no arms.

Close up he looks like old cake
his shoulders shedding crumbled chocolate,
his face a slipped scree of icing,
the side broken open to reveal the darker sponge,
a slurred mess weeping, the crust and flake
caught up in his firework hair.

We must feed him every weekend, says my son,
and we do, even the dog, who sniffs his face
then pees on his branched foot.
The Mud Man looks at me through struck flint eyes
and mutters a requiem for you, for me, for us all,
through broken slate teeth.

White Pebble

Tonight, after the bath and the bedtime story,
somewhere in the space between hanging
and folding damp towels, I kneel down. From here
it is barely a breath, a slow tipping forward,
until my forehead rests on the tiled floor.

In our story the children throw down a pebble trail,
escape from the woods and find their way back home.
I fold the corner of the page to mark our place
and smooth the hair from a sleeping face.
Nobody knows how a story ends.

Here's a pocketful of pebbles, and a mountain of crusts.
Here are small white pills to be taken every day.
There's rosemary, that's for remembrance.
I follow your trail to the copse and kneel down,
rest my forehead on a damp carpet of moss.

The Mud Man whispers to me in a dead language.
Noli timere, he hisses. But I am afraid.
I do not know how I got here and I will not pray.

Oblatory

For Beltane we roll up the bluebell carpet
and feed the Mud Man with its ringing tribute.

For Lammas we strip the hedgerows of berries
and stain his lips with a purple sacrifice.

We ram-raid the squirrels' stores at Samhain,
shove cobnuts into his maw like a slot machine.

The first snowdrops of spring are phlegmatic.
Nodding virgin brides slaughtered for Imbolc.

All year I am appellant, devotee, suitor,
appeasing and wooing him with the copse's fruit

and he is my journey's end, my talisman,
my worry beads, rabbit's foot, saint's bone.

I walk from tree to tree, station to station –
oak, beech, holly, sycamore, hawthorn, hazel, blackthorn –

always arriving at this scarred mound of mud
where I kneel and rest my forehead on the ground

and remember another time, another place.
Your first smile. Your lit face.

Camino

Pampas grass shall inherit the earth. Its cream plumes
wave a lazy hosannah from the central reservation,
each panicle loosing a nebulous halo of seeds.
Twenty-first century pilgrims hug the hard shoulder,
kicking up dust with their 'fight the good fight' boots.

Outside the cathedral, a beggar eyes my dictionary,
my good Boden skirt. 'A coin, one little coin'.
Inside, the wax candles in the Lady chapel are gone.
A man grips the bars, feeds the box, flicks a switch.
Ofrenda. Spenden. Donate. Donare. Darowizna.

We whisper, place our hands on the worn stone,
then walk the streets eating ice cream in the rain.
Nobody mentions the last leg, the rocky road to Finisterre,
the end of the world where land and low sun merge
behind a scattering of campfires and rubbish.

We lie in the dark, naked, feeling strangely chaste,
and every five seconds the smoke alarm sheds a little light
until at last I draw the sheet up over both our faces.

The Way of the Cross

The penitents, what are they thinking? Of the goodness of God?
Or Christ it's hot under here, or should I have come on my knees?
They mill in brotherhoods, trying out their satin glory suits.

Some bag and sag at the neck, which reminds me of elephants,
except the ones in white, which remind me of lynchings.
One pulls back his hood and suddenly becomes ordinary.

The front end of the paso emerges to applause.
Hurrah for Christ on a sea of iris and blue-green hydrangeas
carried by thirty Nazarenos with bare or bandaged feet.

The tip of his cross catches on overhead wires.
There's shouting, and swaying, and shuffling back and forth
then they set off down the street like a drunken battering ram.

The thump and crack of the drums gets us in the solar plexus,
and by the time the Virgin appears, wobbling under her canopy,
I'm so thrilled by the shawms, the pipes, bassoons,

the smell of incense and mothballs, the hard sell of the drums,
I am ready to surrender to a brief sense of wonder
and a handful of praise cards and sticky boiled sweets.

De Correctione Rusticorum

I must not sit by a fountain or spring
for I might be drawn into another world.

I must not visit the sacred groves
to consort with saplings in bright blossom.

I must not carry a stone in my pocket.
A stone can be used as a witness.

I must not honour the moths and the mice
with small heaps of grain and fruit

to preserve our crops and save our cloth.
I must work on a Thursday.

I must not be alone in the mountains,
hang laurel at the lintel, or cook with herbs,

predict the future by means of sneezes
or by the flights of small birds,

for vain are all auguries and foretellings
and dreams have deceived many.

I have put away my entrails.
I will enter with the other foot.

Petition

What do we pray for in the first petition?
We pray for things to end, but not like that.
We pray that someone is wrong, but not us.

What do we pray for in the second petition?
We pray for good results.
We pray for a short stay.

What do we pray for in the third petition?
We pray for a normal childhood for our child.
We pray for, basically, a normal childhood.

What do we pray for in the fourth petition?
A donor GFR of eighty per cent or more
and easy plumbing. A surgeon with good hands.

What do we pray for in the fifth petition?
We pray for strength, for ourselves, and others.
We pray for strength to pray.

What do we pray for in the sixth petition?
A morning with clear blue sky, the promise of sun,
for words to come.

Danish Palaces Egg

I conceive a space
the size of my fist

under my liver
or spleen

shielded by my diaphragm,
my spread ribs.

It holds your kidney
which I am keeping warm.

It is priceless
like a Fabergé egg,

pink enamel
on hand-tooled guilloche,

rose-cut diamonds,
crimson velvet lining,

and squeaky
like a dinette booth cushion

in mauve leatherette,
lightly worn.

Admission

Lying on the hospital bed late at night
with the cannula in my arm starting to sting
and a bag shoving fluids into me at a rate
that tightens my wedding ring

I write a letter to you, at home with our son,
and bury it deep in my notebook
between special diets and test results and plans
where only you would look

just in case anything goes wrong.
Up at six, down at eight, out by twelve, recovery till two.
I'm counting hours. It won't be long.
I love you.

They are going to come and wake me in ten minutes.
I examine a spatter of old blood on the wall.
I am preoccupied by the precise arrangement of sheets.
Look after our boy. I know you will.

They say the gift blesses the giver.
Blood pressure, temperature, pulse rate, blood sugar.

Mountain of Heaven

The Mud Man looks like Ben Nevis –
as high as ten St Paul's but without the convenience of a staircase.

The popular tourist path requires modest scrambling ability
and a head for heights. I choose the hard way

to learn the meanings of words: saddle, col, arête, spike.
Barn-dooring on a 'schrund, I understand skyhook

and also the need for a guide. Two humans in a land of stone
chasing the same star, singing the same tune.

This being 'the Ben' I get Kenny, wearing a kilt
and carrying a half-size piano strapped to his back with a seat belt.

Three days it takes us to reach the summit.
Every six hours Kenny puts down the piano and we rest against it

snacking on Kenny's emergency raisins
and examining my growing collection of bruises and grazes.

At the top I rest my Elvis-legs and enjoy an angel's view of Devon
while Kenny sings 'Scotland the Brave', O land of my high endeavour …

Miracle

You'd think they were slipping an opaque stocking
onto the deacon's leg. Sixty denier, maybe eighty. He doesn't look ill,
even smiles in his sleep and shifts slightly to assist them,
his arms crossed over his chest and clutching his gold chain rosary.

In fact he almost glows in the light cast from their halos.
The new leg covers the cut stump of the old, and Fra Angelico
has chosen not to show the body of the Ethiopian,
later dug up and found to bear the deacon's suppurating limb.

There are clues. The halos, of course. The way they both hover
on wisps of cloud. The glass uroscopy flask, the surgical pincers.
These are Cosmas and Damian, patron saints of physicians,
and this is a dream, a miracle, a beautiful picture

but it's not much of an operating theatre, and all I can see
is the one thing we most dread, which is this:
when the surgeon reaches to delicately unclamp
the clamps which close off the flow of blood through the vessels

the body rejects the organ, like a bad bean,
and it blackens before our eyes. No angels attend either scene.

Hats Off!

i.m. Ronald Lee Herrick (1934-2010)

Hats off to Ronald Lee Herrick, the older, more serious one
whose twin brother Richard was dying of kidney disease,
who said 'I had heard of such things, but it seemed in the realm of science fiction',
who was prepared to undergo a 'mutilation procedure',

who spent five and a half hours on the operating table,
whose mother, Marjorie, worked in the George Foss book store on Court Street,
who had reciprocal skin grafts to prove he and Richard were identical,
who said 'I'd had an appendectomy, and I hadn't much liked that',

whose transplanted kidney helped Richard live for another eight years,
who went back to college after just two weeks,
who changed the meaning of primum non nocere,
who taught school for 37 years in Northborough, Massachusetts,

who said, when Richard ordered him home, 'I am here and I am going to stay'
and, with that, quietly led us all into uncharted territory.

The Mud Man is a Heretic

He fasts on a Sunday. He does not join in public worship.
He exists on rain, sticks and mud.

I tell him the Council of Braga takes a dim view of private ascetics,
that he is undermining the authority of the Church,

that he must be more culturally accommodating.
That the search for the hidden mysteries of nature risks blasphemy.

When I demand that he renounce his errors he says nothing.
I tell him he practises magic. I tell him he is anathema.

The Mud Man believes in revelation.
He does not expect to find what he seeks in any cathedral

but out here, under the sky, where the wind skins his temples.
I know this from the way he looks at the stars.

I suspect he takes part in secret ceremonies as one of the elect.
I have seen him smile at the moon.

I tell him I cannot protect him from the Bishops.
I can hear the grinding of their wagons as they roll over the fields

cutting down all who stand before them,
spitting out broken bodies like so much straw.

Lost
14 November 2015

A language, a time zone and many miles away
you are in a hospital bed again.
I am driving from Cap d'Agde to Béziers

marvelling at the cacti, the olives, the vines,
the biblical nature of the terrain
and, far in the distance, the outline of Spain,

the promise of lands unknown
and as night falls the evening puts on such a show
of red at night, shepherds' delight,

crimson and turquoise and ochre and yellow
that the bleached roof tiles and plaster walls of the houses
glow rose pink against Parisian blue.

Yesterday, the Bataclan. Today we grieve
for those we knew, for those we never knew,
for our stranger world,

and for that part of you which once was mine,
so hopefully given, so hopefully received,
so quickly lost and now no good to you.

Fistula

Linus has an arm cat. It purrs day and night
without stroking. When I cup my hand

over the snaked bulge in his forearm
I feel it hum like a turbine.

Linus's arm cat has nine lives
of indeterminate length. Its name is turbulence.

We know about turbulence, me and Linus,
we know interruptions to flow, what it is to be

roistered by breakers in a mad sea,
the strange quiet of the eye of the storm,

standing in a hospital corridor, not knowing
where you are, or where you're going.

And we know reversals, and rejection,
that silent slipping away.

And we know about grief. There are many kinds
and it's not always a person that dies.

What else do we know? How things pass.
We are both learning about acceptance.

Tumba Dios

And on the eighth day God made a farmer
and he carried a car jack and a scaffold pole
and a fourteen inch Husqvarna

and he found the Mud Man in a foxhole
and he took up tools and got biblical on his ass,

jacked up the trunk and sawed it into chunks,
wedged, sledgehammered, hewed with an axe,

booted the startled root stump down the hill,
slung the splits in the loading bay in the Hilux,
filled in the hole with a dozen spadefuls of dirt

then drove over and over the lumpy mound
until it was flat ground.

My mercenary, my advocate, my hero.

There's a spatter of sawdust where we used to sit,
a smear of part-digested sloe berries
but otherwise he's

gone, replaced by an access road.
Sometimes trees are just trees, mud is mud.

A Lexicon of Yellow

From the grand – gold – to the quotidian –
straw, honey, saffron, camel hair, citrine –

and the less obvious shades of urine: pale whey,
milk white, amber, glaucoma-grey,

and rufus, rubeus, rubicundus –
the reds of blood and beetroot and strep rust –

purple like the pee of mad King George, green,
blue as a bluejay's wing, and black as horn.

So, what says the doctor to my water?
I swirl your sample in my matula,

smell it, taste it, hold it up to the light,
heat it to see if it coagulates.

Is it sweet, like the juice of sugar-cane,
or gruel-like, hair-raising, full of semen,

or turbid like an elephant in rut?
I'll read bubbles like the old piss prophets

foretelling the future by simply spinning a wheel.
And if you don't piss at all?

Scaffolding

wash away
unnecessary flesh

purge
with enzymes and detergent

isolate the intricate
internal architecture

coax stem cells
leeched from marrow

or spun from blood
to grow

then seed the matrix
with your cocktail mix

cross your fingers
make a wish

for a windpipe, a bladder,
a kidney

a lifeline
grown in a petri dish

Tomorrow's World

"Who shall live when not all can live?" – The God Committee

Seems like only yesterday we were watching *Tomorrow's World*,
Raymond Baxter in greyscale RPing over the new artificial kidney machine
a Kiil flat-plate parallel-flow with three grooved polyprop boards
sandwiching pressure-tested, hand-stretched sheets of cellophane –
a kind of sci-fi hostess trolley with jump-start wires and dome cloches –
now ready for home installation, needing only a water softener, phone line,
a separate electricity supply and space for enough water to fill a small loch
possibly dictating an extension to your home or a cabin in the garden
and only for a few – the 'worthy', the employable, the first come.

And what will we say in ten or twenty years at some family reunion,
you with your cup-sized implant engineered in a lab or grown in a pig?
Will we remember the itching, the headaches, the days before Teflon,
the stainless steel monster from Lund, the old Kolff-Brighams –
thirty meters of sausage skin wound round a rotating drum –
the man who exsanguinated à la Jackson Pollock in one uncontrolled
spurt, plugging leaks with wax, making up the dialysate bath –
a teaspoon of this, a teaspoon of that, a pinch of magnesium salt –
and, before that, protein-sparse diets, leeches, death.

Sloe Gin

Rise early. Dress warm.
Wear something that covers your arms.

Sing 'baby, don't fear the reaper' under your breath
or something bluesy and bitter by Blind Faith.

So much depends on the weather; pick a dry day.
Pack a bag; it might involve an overnight stay.

Sometimes you find what you need, more or less.
Check your legs for ticks in long grass.

Sloes are defiant fruit, each one hard won.
Walk home the long way, clutching your pot or pan

and sobbing. Guidance. I'd hoped to give you more.
Add sugar and gin. Shake. Store.

Time matures the thing. At least, adds distance.
I sit at the kitchen table, trying to make sense

and pouring a shot of sweet liquor into a glass.
The filtered magenta, sharp and unctuous,

reminds me of sour plum, of undergrowth,
the scrub, the blackthorn, and the hard path.

Acknowledgements

'De Correctione Rusticorum' and 'Mountain of Heaven' first appeared in *Iota: 94*. 'The Mud Man is a Heretic' was shortlisted in the Plough Poetry Prize 2014. 'Miracle' was commended in the Hippocrates Poetry Prize 2014. 'Tomorrow's World' was shortlisted in the Plough Poetry Prize 2017. 'Hats Off!' was longlisted in the Plough Poetry Prize 2017. 'White Pebble' first appeared in *Writing Motherhood*, Seren Books, 2017.

Thanks

My thanks to the kidney teams at Great Ormond Street, Bristol Children's Hospital and Southmead Hospital, Bristol, and especially to Mr Nabil Kadi, my surgeon, and my living kidney donor nurse Heather Atkins. And to my husband, Andy Brodie, who was (and is) brilliant.

In the UK, around 5,000 people are currently in need of a kidney transplant. The average waiting time is two and a half to three years. More than 250 patients died in 2017 waiting for a kidney transplant, due to a shortage of organs.

From spring 2020, all adults in England will be considered potential organ donors, unless they choose to opt out or are in one of the excluded groups.

For more information about kidney transplants and organ donation contact the National Kidney Foundation at https://www.kidney.org.uk

To sign up to be an organ donor after your death, register here: https://www.organdonation.nhs.uk/